# *Father Figures*

autobiographical poems

by Jay Sizemore

Thanks for supporting poetry !

Crow Hollow Books

# *Father Figures*

Published by Crow Hollow Books
Nashville, TN 37075

Copyright © 2014, Jay Sizemore

Manufactured print on demand

10 9 8 7 6 5 4 3 2 1

ISBN 978-1500589530

*For the others out there.*

# Table of Contents

My Father's Face

His memory has faded
like an old photograph
set too long
in the open air.

My father's face
has all but disappeared,
a yellow smudge
behind the wall of glass.

But once we stood
on the bank of some lake,
the water licking the stones
and aching for our feet,

him close behind,
keeping me warm
with his breath on my neck
and his hands on mine,

helping me hold
the fishing pole
as the bobber floated
on the rippling reflection of the sky,

bubbling excitement
as it vanished beneath
and I reeled too fast

so he did it for me.

The fish was wide-eyed,
small and slick,
as it struggled and died
in my unscarred hands.

I carried it home,
that memory of love turned foul:
a dead fish wrapped
in a paper towel.

Sorry

I apologize for ruining your life.
You should have worn a condom.
Should have guilted her into an abortion.
You could have done it yourself
if you didn't have the money:
heated an old wire hanger
with your trusty Zippo
and rummaged it around inside
like you were trying to unlock her door,
the keys a jingling gag in her mouth,
an ignition switch your fist couldn't fix.

You could have waited for that baby bump,
then punched her there,
black out drunk on the Beast,
just blame it on the booze
like you do everything else,
or you could have pushed her
down a few flights of stairs
hoping the fall didn't break
her slim bird's neck,
claiming it was an accident
of slippery cement,
not a panic attack from the fear
of future responsibility.

If the thought of murder and violence
makes you squeamish,
you should have waited until I was born,

delivered me in the back of your car
where you first showed her your dick,
put me in a garbage bag
and dropped me in the river,
listening to my infant screams
disappear into bubbles,


it would be no different
than your mother
putting baby kittens in bread sacks,
tying them to tree limbs
for her husband to shoot
with his double-barreled shotgun—
better than having another mouth to feed.

The fact of abstract absence

Beneath her breast bone
there is pain that's real,
the Tennessee mountains
of Appalachian pain,
pushed up
from buried emotions
in her tectonic soul.

She's cut highways through
the rock and dirt of that pain,
to traverse the ventricular landscape,
to drive past cliffs and hills
hiding faces like forgotten books
in the shadows and shelves
of those unnatural forms.

She's learned to navigate
the treacherous terrain of herself,
to circumvent what hurts,
that deep-seeded ache
even the touch of a hand
won't subdue, that chill
that runs deeper than bones.

She is lost, a mouse
in the walls of a house
without rooms, running circles
around a truth too close to see,
the satellite image from space

a mountainous mosaic of her father,
who died before she could ask
why he never cared to claim her.

## Gerald

gave me his name when it wasn't his to give,
although his paint-stained fingers
must have left some prints in my mind.
There's a haze of memories smeared
over with vaseline, during a time
some friends still recall with a puzzled look
when they bring up that other name,
that wasn't ever mine. Children only
know what their parents call them.

During the memories of those years,
my mother is strangely absent,
appearing in and out of the timeline
like a star from behind the clouds.
My baby sister seemed to never stop screaming,
except in the hushed blue mornings,
when I would crawl under her crib
and drive matchbox cars around the carpet,
the quiet whir of the humidifier
blowing cool mist onto my palms.

He would sit at the table, drenched
in golden light from an overhead lamp,
and he would show me how
an imagination works, turning scribbles
from a pencil on paper, into cartoons,
taking me to see *Star Wars* for the first time.
That was the year of the great blizzard,
snow drifts piled up the sides of the house,

the unfinished basement an open hole
with a white bottom, the sidewalk
a solid sheet of ice that threatened
to feed me to it, my cowboy boots
betraying me again and again
to bruises on my backside.
I remember my mother's laughter,
a sound that seems to usher time forward,
wiping away the haziness of the past,
and leaving me with a pair of boots in the closet,
and no idea where that man is
who wanted to give me his name.

An Elegy for Innocence

When I was six I knew that Santa Claus existed,
and that Christmas, I saw his silhouette
perched on my grandmother's roof, heard
bells jingle as reindeer shuffled their anxious
hooves against the frozen black shingles.

I knew that God watched my every move,
knew my every thought, twisted my heart
like a blood-soaked rag every time
I felt tempted to do wrong. Every dream
imagined, every wish cast towards the stars,
every truth spoken, was formed from purest
yearning and unblemished perception.

A body in a casket was a person asleep
who wouldn't wake up, a reason for people
to cry, a reason to whisper and place flowers
over foreign names. Don't step on graves.

The End were words for bedtime stories,
and words taking a lifetime to learn how to fear.

Jeffrey Lynn

Small towns are the perfect hiding places
for demons. The spaces in between
those with names on the map,
the places where front doors
remain unlocked all night long
and barking dogs mean
a train is coming.

The first house had roaches
in the kitchen drawers
that scattered like a cloud of black eyes
when exposed to the light. It was close
enough to the school that I could walk,
my breath a transient plume
that followed me through winter.

I would be sent alone to the grocery,
to buy milk with the food stamps
and cigarettes with the cash,
sometimes cheating, and getting myself
some Big League Chew
or a candy bar that I would eat
before I got home.

I don't remember him there,
then I remember him there,
my mother's eyes glossed over
with a lustful romanticism,
telling my sister and I

that they said their own wedding vows
together alone, under a canopy of stars.

Soon after, she started third shift,
and was always asleep or gone, leaving us
in the care of a monster
that wore white t-shirts.
When we were not quiet,
he'd wake us up
banging pans in the haunted hours,
make us hold his belt
in our palms at arm's length,
while staring in the mirror
trying not to fall asleep.

----------

He played an acoustic guitar,
fond of singing "Amy, What You Gonna Do?"
and his eyes looked like faded jeans
seen through a fog of Camel smoke.
He tried to teach me Kung-Fu,
table manners, how to gut a squirrel.
One night he took me frog-gigging,
and a snake swam past our boat,
a little metal thing, painted military green,
that threatened to tip over with any movement,
oars swishing us forward through the water
as lightning flickered overhead.

My memories get clouded after the move

to the trailer park, but I remember him laughing
when he forced me to drink whiskey
for a migraine, and I puked.
Bullies chased me home
every day after school,
he said, "stand up for yourself,
be a man," so I blacked some kid's eye.
I remember learning to use the word
"motherfucker" and the way
he questioned me after he heard
me say it to a friend,
but he didn't punish me,
just stared at me like he wanted
to crush my skull with his heel.

We had a window unit air conditioner
without a cover or knobs,
and I liked to shove jacks into the metal grill,
just to watch them frost over with cold.
My stepbrother and I would stay up late
to watch the adult movies on the pay channels,
cultivating a desire we were too young
to understand. We rode our bikes
during a thunderstorm, knowing
that lightning would never strike us.

One night, the news said a train derailed
somewhere nearby, and warnings
were issued about poisonous gas,
keeping me up, staring
out the window by the top bunk,

waiting to see the green vapor
that would kill me,
but it was the dog-kennel screams
that drove us from that trailer.

Life in Morton's Gap

When the tooth fairy still brought me quarters
for the bicuspids under my pillow,
we lived down a street without lines,
without shoulders, in a house with wood floors.
There was no shower, so we took baths,
and when the gas was off, we would heat
pans of water on the stove
to help fill the tub, where I would stay
until my hands were pale and wrinkled.
When the electric was off, we would light candles
and tell ghost stories that made my sister and I
paranoid of faces in the windows.
I would watch the wax drip down
the sides of glass coke bottles, dabbing
it with my finger, marveling at the way
it cooled and hardened into a shell.

The neighbor's boy was always dirty,
in clothes that didn't seem to fit,
but he taught me how to catch things.
We would wade down the creek,
turning over rocks for crawdads,
checking under logs for snakes.
He always had a collection
in his backyard, snapping turtles
in five gallon buckets, submerged
in brown water that smelled
like reptilian sweat. One day we brought
home a copperhead, my mother screamed,

said I was never to go over there again,
and we didn't understand, grew to hate
each other, and threw rocks meant
to split open our skulls.

At seven years old, I was given my first knife,
and a machete, trusted to scour the woods
for poke weed, chopping its thick stems,
stuffing my nose with its tart leafy scent,
and black garbage bags with its ropy sinew.
I dug up a dog, its body writhing
with white squirmy maggots, spilling
from its eyes and mouth, its teeth
shiny white against the dirt caked
into every opening, and I ran
as if it would spring from the earth
and nip at my heels for waking it,
not knowing its ghost was already
living inside the man who shared
my mother's bed.

I wasn't there

but I was there…
trapped in the body
of an eight-year-old child,
my short fingers capable
of sending my toys
to imaginary graves,
but not stopping
the tears
from streaming
down my mother's face,
not stopping the faceless
fist from tangling
in her long blonde curls
and dragging her from my room
and down the hall.

I can still hear her screaming.

I can still hear the voice
of the monster
calling her bitch,
telling her he is going to
get out his knife,
he is going to
cut the baby
out of her guts,
telling her she will never
leave him again.
I can still hear the thud

of his fist in the wall
and the struggle
as she fights her way
back out of the darkness.

Moonlight falling in
through the rectangular windows
of this small trailer
in the Kentucky woods,
my sister and I
curled under the blankets
of our separate bunks
and held our breath,
our immature minds
incapable of knowing
that we could be hearing
the sounds of
our mother about to die.

But the light came on,
and with a flurry of shouts
and sobs we were in the truck
and gone,
leaving the demon
alone to destroy
everything that could be broken.

I was too young.
I couldn't say
don't go back,
I didn't know

my sister's innocence
was under attack,
I didn't know
the words "abuse," "sexual,"
or "victim,"
but I felt
deep down
a sense of wrong.

I'll never understand
why she did it,
believed his apologies and lies,
left me for a year
to live with my grandparents,
while they moved back
into a different trailer
in a different town,

why he was allowed
to hold my baby brother
in his tainted hands.
I wasn't there
but I was.

I'm sorry I wasn't old enough
to know how to load a gun.

Dear Stepfather

I have wished for your death
every day,
I have wished for it,
and yet I feel robbed.

I can't even remember
the last time I saw you,
the last time you spoke my name
or told me to stop
chewing my food
with my mouth open,
the last time
I saw tears that you made
fall from faces
splash into cupped hands,
yet I have wished for your death.

Every day,
I have wished for it.

I dreamed of confronting you,
of finding your name and address
in the phonebook,
and making that drive.
I dreamed of showing up at your door,
baseball bat in hand,
maybe a pistol tucked snug
into the back of my pants
like the comforting palm

of a loved one
pushing me onto a stage
and saying don't be afraid.

I have no memory
of your actual voice,
just a distant, hollow echo
of screams that sounded
like dinosaurs caged,
like rabid dogs,
like breaking glass and bones
piercing the fleshy
veneer of happiness,
coming to my restless ears,
not sleeping in my twin-size bunk.

I don't know how you would sound now,
much like I have never
heard the voice of the Devil.

But I wished for your death,
every day,
I wished for it.

You are the reason
I want all of my guitars
to be painted black,
the reason I hate
the thought of pain
inflicted upon innocent eyes,
the reason my sister

and I were never close
and are now closer than ever,
the reason my brother
walks with a haunted stare
full of questions unanswered,
the reason he loves
martial arts and music
though he'll never understand
why,
the reason my mother
clutches to family
like a deflating life raft,
a wall full of photos,
none containing your face.

You are the reason
I will never live in a trailer.

For years,
I have carried this hate.
For years,
I have felt like a book
with missing pages.
For years,
I have wanted
nothing more
than to bury a knife
to the hilt
in the cartilage of your sternum
while screaming your name.

For years,
I have wanted an end,
a closure,
a deep sigh of relief
like the sound
of a stone lid
sliding off a well,
looking down to find
a dark pool of reflections,
my face and the sun.

For years,
I have wished for your death.
Every day,
I have wished for it.

But today,
when I heard
that you died
on January the 13th,
most likely alone
and of cancer
in the hospice ward
of a nursing home,
today when I found
that my wish
had finally come true,
nothing happened.

Nothing happened.
Nothing happened.
Nothing happened.

Repression

Memories like that never seem to go away,
even if you burn all the pictures,
even if you cut him out of the ones
you couldn't afford to let go
for fear of forgetting the good parts
of raising your third child.

He had nothing he could want to forget,
but in his mind, the absence of a past
he might prefer to erase was the problem.

It's hard to know who you are,
without an idea of who you could have been.

Twenty-two years later, and that idea was dead.

I felt the relief of years stacked against
a closed closet door slip through the cracks
in my basement floor so I could look inside it,
pull the chain that turns on the bare bulb,
and see that the monster was gone,
though his claw mark scars would always remain
where the beast had struggled for decades
to scratch its way free from its cage.

But that same door I could finally open,
was for him forever sealed shut,
closed up like a tomb with stones
too heavy to lift, buried by the weight

of the years of an entire life without a face
to attach to a feeling of emptiness,
a feeling of loss locked up inside him
like a well without a bottom.

So, we decided to visit the grave.

I don't know how you say good-bye
to someone you never knew,
I went to put my pain at the foot
of the headstone like a bouquet of black roses,
while I think he wanted to let go
of hating something he could not touch.

We rode with a cousin neither of us really knew,
in a truck crowded with squeaky noises
and reminders of childhood tragedies
around every bend in the road
like some kind of ambush
set by a ghost,

pictures in the frame of the windshield glass
haloed with the luminescence of memory
and a mixed bag of feelings,
like swallowing a thumb tack
coated in honey.

We walked to the marker
and read his name,
set in the finality of stone,
but somehow it still seemed fake.

The inscription asked a Lord
to take his hand,
but no god would have ever
allowed such a man to live.

There was silence, under a gray January sky,
a light mist of rain adding an extra chill
to the wind of late afternoon,
as we stood, smoking cigarettes,
not knowing what to say,
but feeling it anyway.

He says he feels like breaking something,
wishes he could dig him up,
just so he could shit in his casket,
but instead he takes one of the decorations,
a clear plastic guitar, and puts it in his pocket.

We start back to the truck cause it's getting late,
and I let them get ahead of me,
I spit on the grave, whisper "fuck you,"
feeling grateful for once that my brother
never got the chance to call you his father.

He's in the ground and I am not

Because he's in the ground and I am not,
I should see the beauty this life can bring,
and put those thoughts in the earth to rot.

The dead stay with us like cold blood clots,
their memory comes like winter's cruel sting,
but still, he's in the ground and I am not.

The things he did to us might still haunt
my thoughts like scars and wake me from dreams,
but I've put those thoughts in the earth to rot.

Time has changed me, but I've not forgot
the broken mirrors, the knives, the nightly screams,
but still, he's in the ground and I am not.

He forged my anger with the words he taught
through hot fists of fear his demons would sing
but I've put those thoughts in the earth to rot.

The devil inside him would have fought
to turn me against myself, to make my heart mean,
but since he's in the ground and I am not,
I've placed those thoughts in the earth to rot.

My mother's déjà vu time machine


The day he left was a day blurred by tears,
a day of hugs good-bye, faces pressed into chests,
a smell of sweat and Old Spice fading into exhaust
and a trail of gravel dust, a day of using children
as guilt-laden bargaining chips, minds unable
to fathom the complex goings on of giants.

It was a day of "I'm sorry" and "how could you"
and as soon as it was over, I stole his Zippo lighter
from the hutch drawer, the one she bought him
for his birthday that he never carried because
he didn't want to ruin it, and she planned
to have it engraved. Since that day, it's worn
my pockets thin.

*clink-clack, clink-clack*
open, closed---open, closed

He gave her a little something to make her feel better,
was what she said, but that Christmas,
the one after the divorce of his replacement,
she behaved like someone best suited for
paper slippers and a hospital gown,
an amnesia patient missing nine years.

That trailer set just beyond  the crest of a hill,
out that damned curvy stretch of road
that sliced right through two seas of green weeds,
its brown and white siding a subdued image of normalcy,
like a wall repainted to hide evidence from new buyers,
still needing its second coat.

The front porch was as inviting as a shark's mouth,
an obstacle course of shadows and uncertainty,
white chairs waiting to be thrown into the yard,
a silhouette with slouched shoulders
watching through the storm door,
while she hugged us,
all cigarette smoke and glossy eyes.

This was the man she returned to,
this peddler of cherry-picked memories,
this collector of diet soda cans,
this toothless trader of howls,
this grizzled skeleton with yellow-
tipped fingers, missing most its insides,
sunken eyes magnified into tiny skies
behind thick prescription glasses.

His smile was all tongue and gums,
asking us to reminisce.
*clink-clack, clink-clack,*
open, closed---open, closed

It was unfair to us that he should be
the coin shuffled beneath
these ten wooden cups,
for her to find whenever she pleased,
while she stole every other man's dollar
who wished to buy a chance
to end the game forever.

She makes the rules up as she goes.

So here we were, back in this haunted double-wide,
the pallid ghost of Christmas Past wrapped in the
threadbare chains of his flannel frailty,
a graveyard fog of second-hand smoke acting like vaseline
rubbed on a camera lens to take us back in time,
down a road littered with rusted detour signs and warnings
written in faded lettering that read "No Exit,"
a path meant to help us forget:

that possible affair with
her brother's wife,
the job that he just never
could seem to find,
the feud with her parents
and his refusal to seek the Lord,
the woman he left at the hospital
emergency room door,

who nearly OD'd on painkillers.

*clink-clack, clink-clack*
open, closed---open, closed

I've never been so embarrassed to be alive,
to see my mother slurring her words
as she blesses the food, rocking from side to side,
her hand clinching mine like I'm a life raft
and she's swimming the ocean,
as she thanks "baby Jesus" for bringing us all together,
and I find it hard to restrain my laughter and my rage.

Two months later, and that fog was gone from her eyes,
after she realized his nostalgia was a job that would never
offer medical, while those rectangular discolorations
in my front pockets' denim seemed more and more
a symbol of useless metal without the fuel
needed to start a fire. So, I threw that weight
from my palm, into the woods behind my house.

Two years later, she's added two more wooden cups
to her table top con, and I came home to find
his truck parked in her drive.

*Clink.*

Seventeen

When I worked at my dad's restaurant,
my hands smelled like onions,
my hair smelled like onions,
my sweat smelled like onions,
such a tart, burning odor,
it kept me awake at night.

The world seemed smeared with a coat of grease,
smudged around the edges, dingy brown,
even after two showers, I felt like a hamburger
squished under a press, my skin a sizzle-pop
mess of burning fat on the grill of adolescence.

One night I served a bully
a handful of my pubes
mixed in with his taco salad,
and I thought about how it felt
to sit on the edge of my dad's bed,
the loaded .38 in my hands,
thinking of reasons to keep living.

hindsight blurry

I should write a happy poem, but I don't know how.
Everything I say feels like a lie.
Spoiler alert: everything is fucked because of money.
The first night I stayed in your house
there was a porno left in the VCR;
I stayed up past dawn, jerking off.
The family business was a grease pit,
so I stopped washing my hair.
My mother got drunk and pretended to be a pirate.
Hearts were made from fistfuls of cashews.
A rectangle scar in the side of your head
where they sucked the black blood off your brain.
Loaded pistol in the top drawer,
pink dildo kept in the bottom.
How many days I wished to be someone else.
A Freemason symbol on one hand,
a lion on the other,
neither clasped in prayer,
neither bunched in curls of blonde hair.
Left like Tin Man to rust in the rain.

Repeating mistakes

I knew divorce was on the horizon
when her face took on that look
of translucent skin stretched
over the skull of a goldfish,
her mouth a dark circle of exhaustion.

She said he was a horrible, repulsive man,
someone who would rather clean his guns
than clean himself, a native of the forest
of couch cushion and unwashed clothes,
pale blue eyes vacant of dignity

telling her he would give her spending money
if she would suck his cock once a week.

There was that brick house,
with the picturesque tree and the wind chime,
the basement he wanted to kick my brother out of,
threatening to strangle him with a Metallica t-shirt,
while the hunting channel showed pictures
of deer perking their ears up in the background,
oblivious to the cross hairs.

I imagined him crawling on top of her
in the middle of the night,
his tongue like a slimy tobacco leaf,
his matted hat hair plastered to his scalp,
his beer gut pressing down into her lungs,
as he used her mouth for his spittoon,

drowning her screams in brown juice.

On her nightstand there was a photograph
of him and her with her first turkey kill,
both of them in matching orange vests and camo,
behind them a thicket of wild branches
and broken bits of gray winter in between,
them holding up the plumage of tail feathers,
smiles not revealing any secrets
that the colors of the world would wish to keep,
and two years later, she forgot she told them.

Queen Bee planning her father's funeral

She walks in a swarm of imaginary bees,
their whirring wings a buzz like tinnitus,
something to talk over, an auditory fog
that blends words to fill in the gaps
with antonyms of cognitive dissonance.

She sweats a Vaseline sheen,
a happy honeysuckle scent, secreted
from hexagonal glands, wringing her hands
through the coffee mug's ear, as she slips
from skin to skin, pretending to smile.

Her father, the straw man she puts a match to,
but every day he survives the flame, Moloch in reverse,
and it hurts, the waiting, the inevitable loneliness
that cannot be acknowledged. Instead, she celebrates
every breath as if his next will never come,

while building a coffin for each one
of the worker bees in her hive,
devouring the honey
of manufactured happiness
from her body, the tree trunk.

Playing with railroad cars

We were warned not to place rocks on the tracks,
for the train might derail.
In my mind I saw a giant steel dragon,
fire and smoke spewing from its nostrils
as it thundered and careened down
the embankment of white stones
after those who would dare
disrupt its path with pebbles.

To know if a train was coming,
we would press our ears
to the sun-warmed metal
of the rails, those thick beams
of reflective light holding our tiny silhouettes
as we crouched and listened and felt
for the dull hum of its approaching weight and momentum.

Once we knew, our dirty hands would be fishing
our pockets for the nickels, pennies, and dimes,
brought to be smashed to smithereens,
just because, because we wanted to dance
with the power of destruction,
that giant beast we heard scream every night,
like a lonesome monster enslaved.

*Plink, plink, plink....*
our coins would go against the steel
in haphazard lines, the train already breaching the horizon,
and our hearts would flutter like moths trapped in lamp shades
as we cascaded down the hill of treacherous stones
into the tree line, never fearing the dangers of twisted ankles.

Within moments the air was full of sound,
an energy like a storm of colossal wheels,
churning and cranking, pushing and driving,
whistle howling its torturous howl
as the cars *clickity-clacked* and weighed
the tracks rhythmically up and down
like the hyper tense arteries of god pumping steel
instead of blood.

Some coins were forever lost among the myriad of gravels,
but others we found, pulverized into odd shapes like putty,
president's faces stretched or gone, words illegible,
hardly recognizable as coins at all.

We never thought about the homeless man who died,
passed out drunk on the tracks,
just weeks earlier, though they say his head was never found,
we took our souvenirs and watched the dragon's tail slide up
the mountain.

# Acknowledgements

Many of these pieces were first published in online or print journals, and I give my thanks and gratitude to the editors who took chances on my work.

"My mother's déjà vu time machine," appeared in *Waterhouse Review*, October 2012.

"The fact of abstract absence," appeared in *Big River Poetry Review*, August 2012.

"Seventeen," appeared in *Words Dance*, June 2013.

"Repeating mistakes," appeared in *Cease, Cows*, June 2013.

"Playing with railroad cars," appeared in Black Heart Magazine, January 2014.

"Sorry," appeared in *Luciferous*, January 2014.

"I wasn't there," "The bad dream," "Repression," and "He's in the ground, and I am not," appeared in the anthology *Beyond the Dark Room*.

Jay Sizemore flunked out of college and has spent his life enslaved to corporate America. This has rewarded him with many tales of woe. He still sings in the shower. Sometimes he writes his songs down. His work has been published in numerous online and print journals, such as *Red River Review, Lunch Ticket, Prick of the Spindle, Words Dance, DASH*, and *Still: The Journal*. Currently, he works as Poetry Editor for *Mojave River Press and Review*. He lives in Nashville, TN, home of the death of modern music.

Made in the USA
Charleston, SC
27 September 2014